SPORTS CODING CONCEPTS

SPORTY ALGORITHMS

Allyssa Loya

Lerner Publications ◆ Minneapolis

Lerner Publications Company
An imprint of Lerner Publishing Group, Inc.
241 First Avenue North
Minneapolis, MN 55401 USA

For reading levels and more information, look up this title at www.lernerbooks.com.

Main body text set in Mikado a Regular.
Typeface provided by HVD Fonts.

Library of Congress Cataloging-in-Publication Data

Names: Loya, Allyssa, author.
Title: Sporty algorithms / Allyssa Loya.
Description: Minneapolis, MN, USA : Lerner Publications, [2020] | Series: Sports coding concepts | Includes bibliographical references and index.
Identifiers: LCCN 2019011840 (print) | LCCN 2019016211 (ebook) | ISBN 9781541583627 (eb pdf) | ISBN 9781541576919 (lb : alk. paper)
Subjects: LCSH: Computer algoritims—Juvenile literature. | Sports—Juvenile literature.
Classification: LCC QA76.9.A43 (ebook) | LCC QA76.9.A43 L677 2020 (print) | DDC 005.1—dc23

LC record available at https://lccn.loc.gov/2019011840

Manufactured in the United States of America
1-46710-47704-6/20/2019

Table of Contents

SPORTS AND ALGORITHMS

Lines of code are instructions that tell a computer what to do. An algorithm is more than one line of code put together. Once you understand algorithms, you'll see them everywhere—especially in sports! Imagine players on a soccer team passing the ball to one another. Each pass is like a line of code. All the passes put together are like an algorithm. Coding is easy when you think about it like that!

Use algorithms to score points and learn new sports moves! You'll need plain paper, construction paper, dice, a pencil, a ruler, scissors, and a small stuffed animal for some of the activities.

TAKE THE SHOT!

You need to move your body in the right order to shoot a basketball. Each move is like one line of code. All the moves together are like an algorithm.

Get a partner and pretend you are a coach. Your partner is a player. Look at the moves on page 7. Decide what order the moves should be in to shoot a basketball. Say them aloud. Your partner will act out the moves as you say them and pretend to shoot a ball. Watch to see if the order of the moves makes sense. If not, reorder the moves and try again. You can check your answer on page 29.

Throw the basketball.

Bend your knees.

Watch the ball go through the hoop!

Aim for the basket.

HOME RUN HERO

Your teammate just hit a home run! He has to run around the bases to home plate. Look at the baseball field on the next page. Then look at the arrows below the field. Each arrow is an instruction, or line of code.

On your own paper, use the arrows to write an algorithm. The algorithm should tell your teammate to run around the bases. Go from home plate to first base, second base, third base, and back to home plate. Run, or start, the algorithm. Trace each step with your finger on the baseball field. Did your algorithm work? If not, try again.

TEAMWORK

In soccer, moving the ball down the field can be tricky. Each step must stay away from defenders. If not, the other team may take the ball.

Look at the soccer field on the next page. Think about moving from the Start square to the Shoot! square. Trace the path with your finger, and count the squares. Write an algorithm on your own paper using arrows. The algorithm should instruct the player to move from the Start square to the Shoot! square. Be sure to avoid the defenders. Run your algorithm to see if it works.

defender

TOUCHDOWN!

Things often go wrong in sports. Players miss shots or drop balls. People make mistakes when writing algorithms too. If an algorithm has bugs, or mistakes, it won't work. A computer won't be able to follow the instructions.

Look at the football field on the next page. Then look at the algorithms below the field. Run them to try to move the football to score a touchdown. Two of the algorithms have bugs. The bugged algorithms cause the football to run into a defender. Choose the algorithm that stays away from defenders and scores a touchdown!

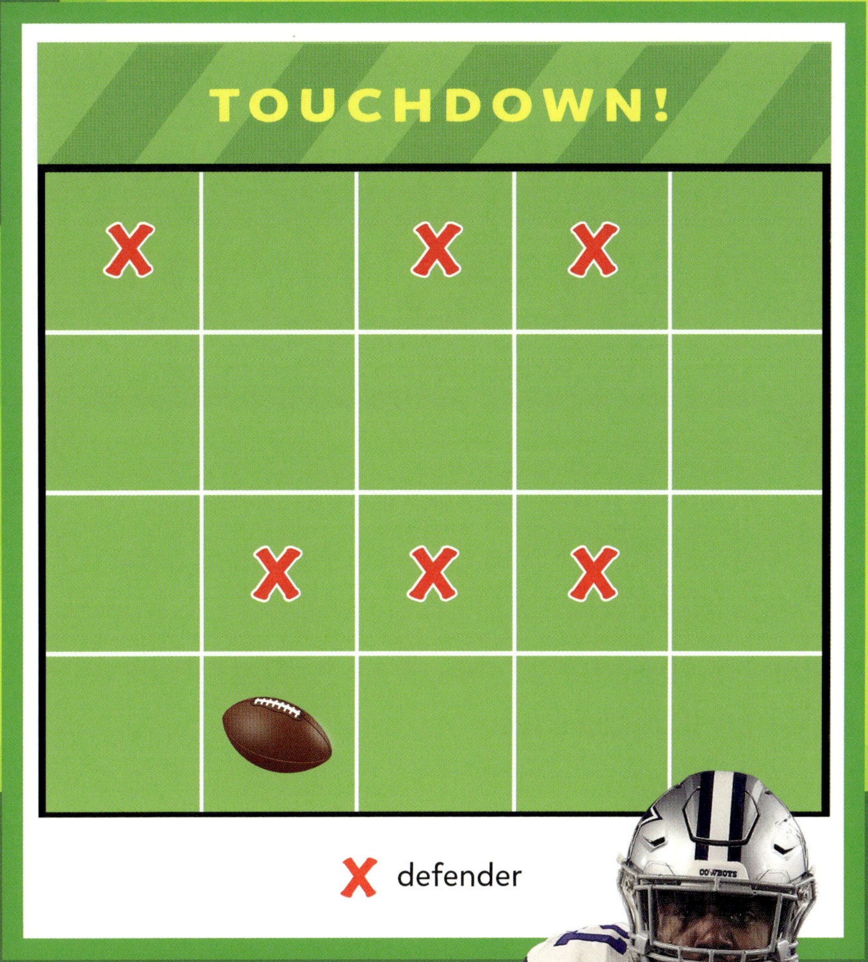

A. ← ↑ →

B. ← ↑ ↑ → → → ↑

C. ← ↑ ↑ → ↑ ↑

RUN LIKE THE WIND

Runners jump over hurdles in some track-and-field races. A runner must leap at the right time to jump a hurdle. If the runner jumps at the wrong time, she'll hit the hurdle and probably lose the race.

Look at the algorithms below each track on the next page. Two of the algorithms are bugged. If there is a hurdle, the line of code below it must tell the runner to jump. If there is no hurdle, the code should tell the runner to run. Choose the runner who will win the race!

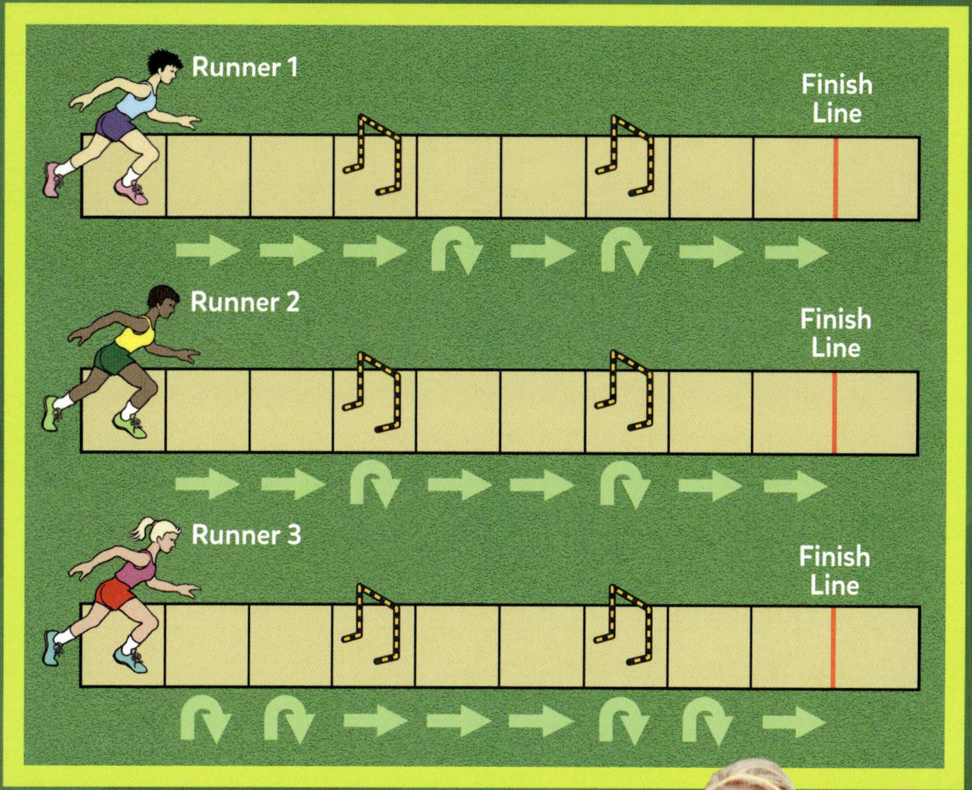
Runner 1
Finish Line
Runner 2
Finish Line
Runner 3
Finish Line

run

jump

TAKE IT TO THE HOOP

It's easy to score points in basketball when you're close to the basket. But it can be hard to get there. You have to avoid defenders as you dribble the ball.

Draw a basketball court on your own paper like the one on the next page. The court should be a 4 by 4 grid. A ruler can help you make straight lines. Draw a basketball in the lower-left square of your court. Write "Shoot!" in the top two center squares. Put a defender in three of the blank squares.

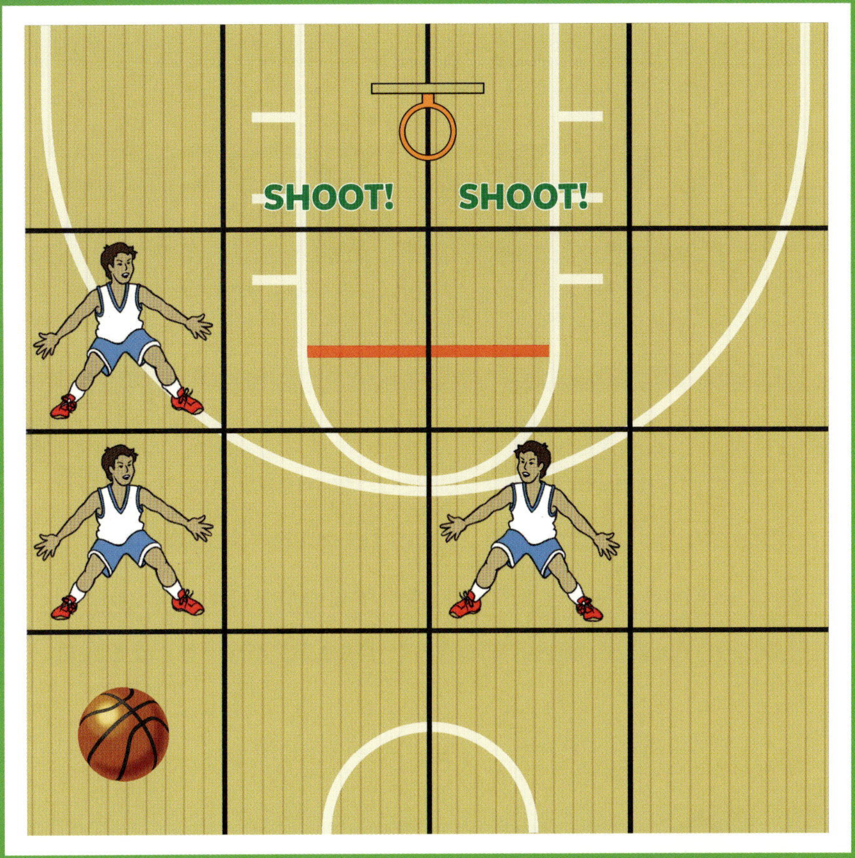

Use arrows to write an algorithm below your court. The algorithm should instruct the ball to move to one of the Shoot! squares. Run the algorithm. It has a bug if the ball runs into a defender. Fix, or debug, the algorithm and run it again. Then draw a new court, put the defenders in different squares, and try another algorithm!

GYMNASTICS FUN

A gymnast might repeat a move many times. You can use loops to give the same instruction many times in an algorithm. Loops tell a computer how many times to repeat a step.

An algorithm to tell a gymnast to flip five times looks like this:

flip, flip, flip, flip, flip

The same algorithm with a loop looks like this:

5(flip)

The number says to take the action five times. The looped algorithm is faster and easier to write.

A gymnastics algorithm with loops could be 4(cartwheel), 3(flip), 2(forward roll). That tells a gymnast to do four cartwheels, three flips, and two forward rolls. On your own paper, write a gymnastics algorithm using loops. Use moves such as flip, forward roll, cartwheel, handstand, twist, and others. Run the algorithm using a stuffed animal. Make the stuffed animal do the moves as you read them.

GET THE PUCK!

Hockey players hurry to control the puck. Help them get there fast!

Look at the hockey rink on the next page. The puck is in the upper-left corner. The player in the lower-right corner is going to use this algorithm to get to the puck:

↑↑↑←←←←↑

Write a new, faster algorithm. Remember that loops are faster than writing each line of code. You can take any path to the puck, but don't run into the goal. Go to page 29 to see one possible answer.

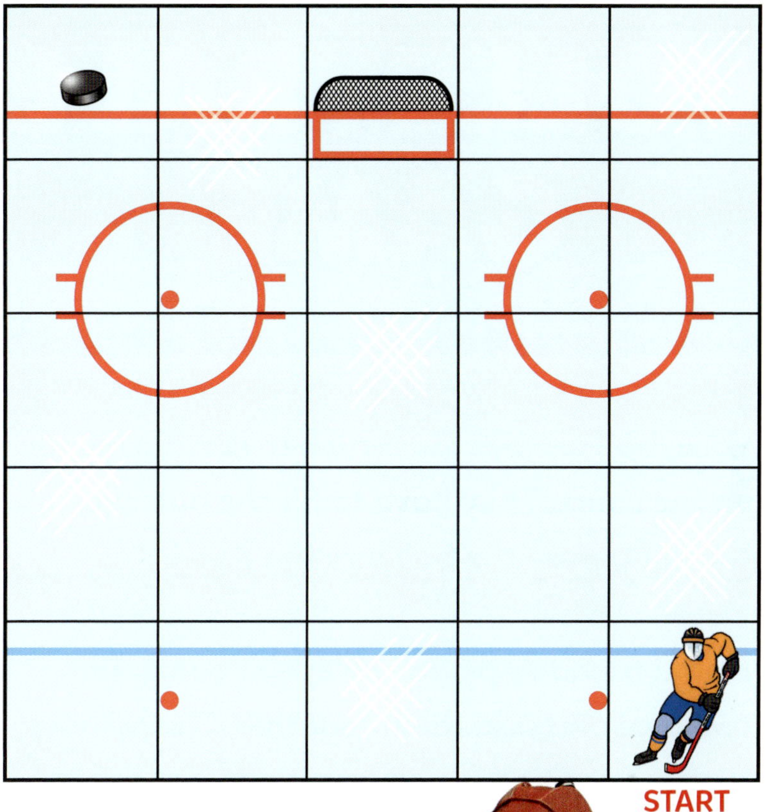
START

VOLLEYBALL GAME

Volleyball players must rush to certain places on the court. They have to hit the ball over the net before the ball hits the floor.

Find a friend to play a volleyball game. Roll two dice and add them together. The number is where the ball is going to land on the grid on page 23. You and the other player will each write an algorithm. Use arrows to go from the Start! square to the number on the grid. Whoever writes a correct algorithm first gets a point. Remember that using loops is faster than writing out each step of an algorithm. Play until someone gets five points.

9
10
11
12
8
7
6
5
START!
2
3
4

VROOM, VROOM!

Drivers zoom around tracks as fast as they can to win auto races. They must also avoid crashing into other cars.

Look at the racetracks and cars on the next page. Help the race car drivers by writing algorithms with loops that will get the drivers across the finish line. The algorithm has a bug if a car crashes into another car. Race to the finish line by seeing how fast you can write bug-free algorithms! You can even use a timer to keep track of your speed.

Track 1

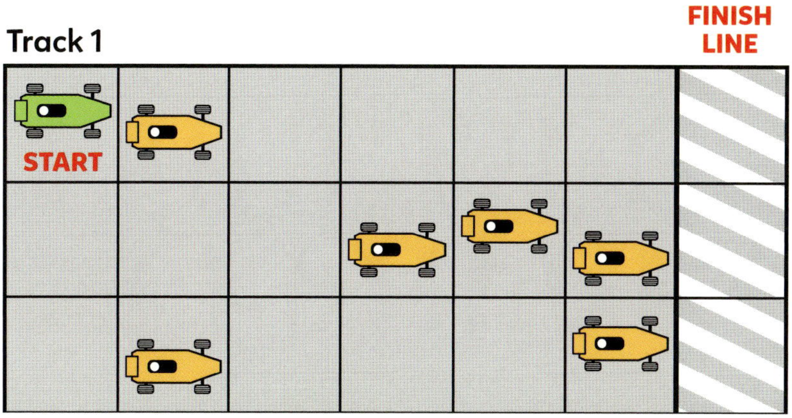

Track 2

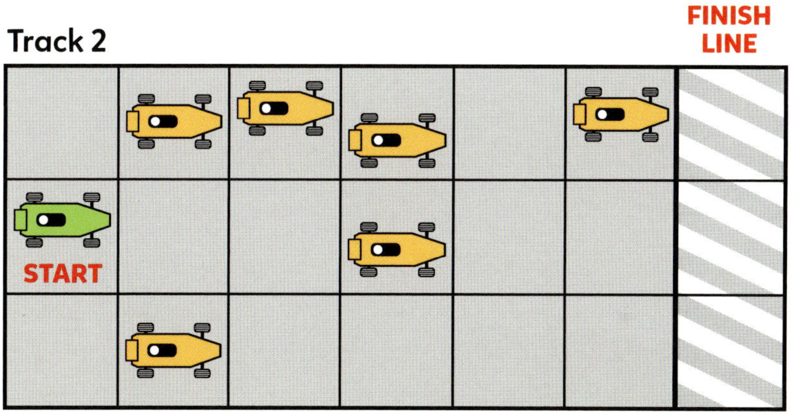

Track 3

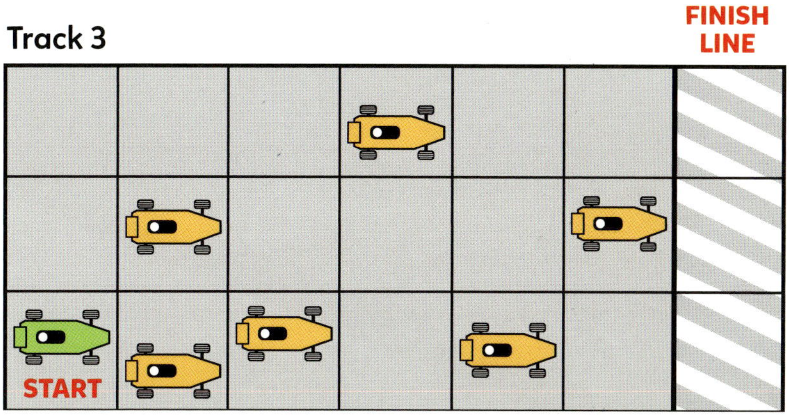

DOWNHILL DANGER

Skiing is fun if you stay on the trail. If not, you can run into trees or rocks! Make your own trail, and then write an algorithm to ski down it.

Use a ruler to draw a 5 by 4 grid on a sheet of construction paper. It should look like the example at the bottom right of this page. Cover the whole sheet of construction paper with the grid. Cut along the lines to make 20 squares of paper.

Line up the squares to create a trail like the one you see below. You can use as many squares as you like. Add at least one turn in the path. Then write an algorithm with loops to ski down the trail. The algorithm is bugged if you go off the path. Debug it and run it again. Set up new trails with different twists and turns!

Keep Coding!

Learning about algorithms might help you see them everywhere, especially in sports. The next time you are watching or playing a game, think about algorithms. How many times did you dribble the basketball? Throw a football, and think about the steps you took. Is the order of the steps important? Try writing algorithms for moves your favorite players make on the field. Use loops to speed up your algorithms!

You can do fun activities on your own to practice algorithms. Write an algorithm for a football play, and ask your friends to help you run it. Help someone learn to throw a baseball by thinking about each move. Break down the moves into step-by-step instructions. Run the algorithm, and let the ball fly. Soon you'll be an all-star at writing algorithms!

Answer Key

Pages 6–7: Aim for the basket. Bend your knees. Throw the basketball. Watch the ball go through the hoop!

Pages 8–9: → ↑ ← ↓

Pages 10–11: ← ↑ ↑ →

Pages 12–13: C

Pages 14–15: Runner 2

Pages 20–21 (possible answer): 2(↑) 4(←) 2(↑)

Pages 24–25: ↓ 2(→) ↑ 4(→), 2(→) ↓ 4(→), 2(↑) 2(→) ↓ 2(→) ↑ 2(→)

Glossary

algorithm: a group of instructions, made up of lines of code, that tells a computer how to solve a problem or finish a job

bug: a mistake found in lines of code

code: instructions for computers that are written in a way that computers can follow

debug: to fix a mistake (a bug) in a line of code

dribble: in basketball, to bounce the ball on the floor as you move with the ball

hurdle: a barrier runners must jump over during races

loop: a line of code that tells the computer to repeat an instruction a certain number of times

pass: move the ball or puck from one teammate to another

run: to start a program

Further Information

CodeMonkey
https://www.playcodemonkey.com

Code.org
https://code.org/learn

Funk, Josh. *How to Code a Sandcastle*. New York: Viking, 2018.

Lyons, Heather. *Coding to Create and Communicate*. Minneapolis: Lerner Publications, 2018.

Lyons, Heather, and Elizabeth Tweedale. *Learn to Program*. Minneapolis: Lerner Publications, 2017.

Prottsman, Kiki. *My First Coding Book*. New York: DK, 2017.

Index

Photo Acknowledgments

Image credits: Laura Westlund/Independent Picture Service, throughout (illustrations); MakiEni's photo/Getty Images, p. 4 (left); Bombaert Patrick / EyeEm/Getty Images, p. 4 (right); KathyDewar/Getty Images, p. 5 (gymnast); gurineb/Getty Images, p. 5 (football player); master1305/Getty Images, p. 5 (volleyball player); Lightspring/Shutterstock.com, p. 6; amriphoto/Getty Images, p. 7 (shoes); FatCamera/Getty Images, p. 7 (athlete); Cavan Images/Getty Images, p. 7 (hoop); Cavan Images/Getty Images, p.7, (basketball); TerryJ/Getty Images, p. 8; Rinek/Getty Images, p. 9; Lazi & Mellenthin/Getty Images, p. 10 (left); DragonImages/Getty Images, p. 10 (right); Hirun Laowisit/EyeEm/Getty Images, p. 10 (left); undefined undefined/Getty Images, p. 12; Michele Constantini/Getty Images, p. 12 (left); Sean M. Haffey/Getty Images, p. 13; VacharapongW/Getty Images, p. 14; Paul Blackley/Getty Images, p. 15; Compassionate Eye Foundation/Steve Coleman/OJO Images Ltd/Getty Images, p. 16; Suriyo Hmun Kaew/EyeEm/Getty Images, p. 16 (right); Rubberball/Erik Isakson/Getty Images, p. 18; Grant Faint/Getty Images, p. 18 (right); DSGpro/Getty Images, p. 20; Score/Aflo/Getty Images, p. 21; irin-k/Shutterstock.com, p. 22; Photodisc/Getty Images, p. 23; Michael Burrell/Getty Images, p. 24 (left); Dave Reginek/Getty Images, p. 24 (right); TIZIANA FABI/Getty Images, p. 26.

Cover: Lazi & Mellenthin/Getty Images, (soccer ball); Blend Images/Pete Saloutos/Getty Images, (football player); Matt_Brown/Getty Images, (volleyball); Shoji Fujita/Getty Images, (baseball player); Suriyo Hmun Kaew/EyeEm/Getty Images, (basketball); Jorg Greuel/Getty Images, (design).

About the Author

Allyssa Loya is an elementary school librarian in North Texas and is the author of the Disney Coding Adventures series. Loya has two young boys and is married to an IT manager, who is a perfect support system for her technological endeavors.